Court -
Thank you for the
love + support.

73

Lessons on Being Tenderheaded

 CB

by Janae Johnson

Write Bloody Publishing

writebloody.com

First edition.
ISBN: 978-1949342413

Cover Design by Janae Johnson
Cover Photo by Christian Eddings
Interior Layout by Winona León
Edited by Wess Mongo Jolley and Sam Preminger
Proofread by Wess Mongo Jolley and Sam Preminger
Author Photo by Zorn B. Taylor

Type set in Bergamo.

Printed in the USA

Write Bloody Publishing
Los Angeles, CA

Support Independent Presses
writebloody.com

LESSONS ON BEING TENDERHEADED

LESSONS ON BEING TENDERHEADED

FOREWORD

By Amber Flame

It is a rare gift to witness a book coming into being up close & personal. The evolution of each & every one of these poems, of the poet herself, was a magic that could not resist splitting me & my own writing open in response. I feel intimately partnered with these poems, a hopeful doula in the birthing process.

In the poetry world, the word "accessible" is often a dirty one, as if striving for an oblique remoteness in relationship to the audience is some proof of value. *Lessons On Being Tenderheaded* is a collection that intuitively seeks out its own, holds out a hand & asks us to understand. How refreshing, to fall repeatedly into the story of this girlchild, this certain kind of woman, as she is challenged to name herself again & again. Here are stories about Black people, written in reverence of Black people, & it is easy to imagine this book in their hands, well-worn & thumbed through, pages of mirrors where we can see ourselves lovingly portrayed & whole.

It wasn't so long ago that Black queer masculine-of-center stories were non-existent in representation. As Janae reflects in 'Pedagogy', your best hope was to elicit coded knowledge from a random encounter. Here exists a growing body of work that captures the turmoil in discovering who & what you are, in the absence of a role model or example, & in a sudden, sometimes violent, 'Initiation'. We are in a time when this work joins others in deepening the conversation around queer identity outside the white gaze, & around relationships of all sorts when they have divested of heteronormative standards. What is a daughter, dressed in her brother's clothes & looking more like her mother every day, but her own whole & natural self? This is for the ones who have looked for the record of their history in vain. Janae has documented here the story of those who, in the words of Lucille Clifton, have shaped themselves into a kind of life with no model before them.

Character-driven, this body of work often finds itself on the basketball court, where the game is both a lens through which self in relationship to community is implacably examined, & a metaphor for the impermanent & shifting nature of our own cherished beliefs through the progression of time. Have no doubt Janae has done her work. She studied the words of her poetic forebears & contemporaries, dissecting resonance & harmonic overtones like a composer. This poet clearly has a profound love for music— it pours out in easy lyricism, innate rhythm, & natural reference— & like any good concept album that's best listened to in order from track one to the end, this book pulls you along a hero(ine)'s journey until we land, together, happier in our own skin.

No One Said Don't Shoot

I remember how young I was when the world opened
fire, a boy with his fingers held like a handgun,
elbow locked & loaded, one eye open. I remember
how softly his mother shushed the imaginary
violence, this perhaps four year old— definitely
couldn't have been much older than me.
& I always wondered
if he was ever punished at home, or where he learned to chew,
aim, cock & spit a word like that on a Saturday afternoon.
I remember it was around that age when we no longer lived
in Oakland & everyone began telling me
how pretty my name was & asked where I got it
from, like it was a winter coat or an honest gold chain.
& I probably shrugged before they suggested it was French
It's gotta be & began adding a 'z' to the front
or a closed-tooth rumble like a car turning over—
hoping to make me sound exotic or un-Black
& I remember this, because I did not have the heart
to tell them *it ain't that deep* or, how my mama just plain
named me after another Black girl, who was ten years older
& used to babysit me before we moved. I am pretty sure
it had to be around pre-school because my new
next door neighbor asked if I ever had a crush before
& when I said 'Janae,' she almost choked on her Capri Sun
because she thought I meant myself.
& I remember this fondly because I was at the age where
both could have been true.

& this was around the time of my first ever Basketball game
        which happened on accident,
because it rightfully belonged to my brother.

Story goes—
when a boy got hurt in the fourth quarter
his coach scans the spectators, in an act of desperation
cuffs a hand— his voice, a slight fracture,
while hollering, *can anyone play?*
& here I come,
galloping down the bleachers,
hair barrettes clacking like rattling branches,

in my Janae-loving skin
with hands on hips, feet shoulder-width apart, knuckles clenched
& an all-too-serious straight face, responding to the coach's bottom lip
I'm ready!
Then, the game recommences on the whistle.
      & this likely preceded the same next door neighbor warning me
      to never share my crushes with anyone else again.
Anyway, I unzip my blocked hot pink & turquoise Reebok
windbreaker to reveal there are indeed shorts underneath
& coach rummages to pull an extra jersey from his duffle bag
which fits me like an oversized t-shirt
doubled as a nightgown.
      Yes, must have been young
      because there was very little outrage over
      what the sag in my uniform must imply.
Story goes, when I entered the game I missed every shot
& for the record, I took a lot of shots for a game
that was never mine.
Every attempt swirling, prancing, bankhead bouncing
around the rim.
Even pulled up for a three pointer on a fast break.
Basked in audacity
til the backboard belly-laughed into a coughing fit
& eventually, I joined in on the gag.
      Yeah, sounds about right—
      must have been about five years old
      to have overshot without correction, to have thrown
      myself a party in the middle of a man's game
      without victory to prompt me, without
      their world knowing my name.

RECKLESS, BRANDON

Brandon asks if
I want to be a boy.
Lord no. Often, yes.
A fourth-grade splinter
of a daydream premiered
as my corkscrew coiled scalp
turned gel slick. *Yes lawd.* Black
Richie Rich impersonator. Tailored
suit snark only. Yes, perhaps I wonder
boy things, Brandon. While staining sheets
vengeance red, Brandon. Yes, girl is too pretty
of a name to call myself. I deserve pretty things,
but mostly money. Run it. Are you a girl if there is no

woman you wish to become?

Brandon asks if I want to be a boy. Lord yes. Often, no.
Standing to pee is so reckless it should be unlawful
in California (at the very least). Still, there is a
serenity that only exists within my mother's
perfumes when she is not home. Yes,
perhaps I wonder girl things too,
Brandon. While grabbing my
jeans where a crotch could
have been, Brandon. Boy
is too reckless of a name
to call myself. Though
I deserve ugly things
but— mostly love.
Run it. Are you a
boy if there's no
man you wish
to respect?

LADIES LOVE COOL J
First Day of 8th Grade

Two Finger Kiss   Lip Puff   Peace Sign   FUBU   Yellow   05   On
Back   Sleeveless   Navy   Stripe   *You*   *Know*   *What*   *It*   *Is*   Watch
Watchless Wrists
Check Time
Bell Rang
Called It
Sound Like   Arco Arena   Encore Chant   This Outfit   This   New Fit
No Fitted   No Skull Cap   Braids Tight   Like Locked   Dap   Lick Lips
Peep Shawty
Rub Hands
Head Nod
What Up Doe?
Lip Bite
One Leg Free
Midnight Denim
Rolled To Knee
You See Me

Lip Curl   Chin   Rub   Like Goatee   Like
Grown   Man   *Man*   *When You Gon Ditch*
Yo   *Friends*   *Like*   *When*   *You*   *Gon*
Run   *Away*   *Wit*   *This*   FUBU   05
No   Wrinkle   Touch   It   Mama
Ironed   I   Ain't   Pressed   Be   Cool
Like   LL   Loungin   Album   Shades
Match   These   Shoes   Almost   Match This
FUBU   05   Yall   Fools   Done Seent   The   Commercial   Lip   Pout
Ladies   Love   Me   Dropped   Allowance   Fa   Shawty   To   Catch   My

Pose   Be Still   She Comin   Cross Arms   Arm Hold   Limb Swing
Stay Put   Be Cool
Lick Lips   Look Swole
Swollen   Can't Feel
Too Royal   Can't Catch
Her Gaze   Only If She
Say   Hi   Then   Reply   Be   Like   *Hello*   Oh   Hell   Pretend   You
Ain't   See Her
Pretend   You Def
Jam   Remix   Yo
Face   Kid   Bite Lip
Be Todd   Mr. Smith
Coolin 1-900   Nah   Start   Fresh
Repeat   Like   Time   Be   Free   Like   Tardy   Be   All   You   Gon   Learn

Today   Like   You   Ain't   Eva   Pressed
Like   Whole   School   Betta   Come   Smell
This   Shame   First   This   Chainless   Neck
Lick   Those   Cracked   Lips
Parched   Son   Thirsty   Awe   Shit
Here   Come   Ol Boy   Boyfriend   Eyebrow
Slit   Stay   Blockin   Yo Sun   Got   FUBU
05   With   Sleeves   Think   He   Cold
Black   Cap   Flipped   Air   Force   Ones
Stomped   Now   You   Wrinkled   His   Right   Arm   Wrapped   Around   Yo
Universe   How   You   Get   Schooled   At   School   Look   Up   Kid   You   Late

My Neighbor Nash Say, Part I

One time I carried the rock like a comet. It was
one of those games sweat couldnt touch me or only
grazed my forehead so the cameras could believe
I was real. I put that stank on em like boom-clack
then crossed over, but not too close to my feet.
You know, some people put that thang right in front
of em then wait for others to pick em like groceries. Ha!
Not me. I had a quick cross. I mean I still do, but
back in the day it was like you was followin the wrong
ball the whole time. There was this one dude best believe
was the size of Karl Malones shadow. I aint lie.
Yo big man fell when I hit em wit dat woop-woop.
Swear to Jimmy Dean. He fell like chopped wood
Remember that dude I was tellin you about? Knocked
a ref to the ground? Think he was suspended or kicked
off the team or sumthin. Its easy to lose yourself out
here. This aint no game of the first draft. Come to my
court when that story is complete. You tellin me
you aint got a crossover? You betta off movin to a new
city. Who told you to be so awful? Dont practice on us
dammit. Practice at home then come back. One time
I spent an entire summer without a rim. Ever do that?
Tell me I aint got no imagination. Just made a wish
at the backboard & dealt with it. Ive played defense
til my bones felt like they was crashin out of my knees
but never been responsible for bringin nothin to life
the way I did back den boy. Aint no kid in the world
got a spit of patience no more. They aint gotta work
on creativity. Basketball could fund the arts ya know?
Think about it. Cuz we made the finger roll. The spin
move. We didnt make the hook shot but made it look
pretty didnt we? Ever seen a white guy with a clean
hook shot? Sure Jerry West maybe. But Jerry
was smooth. No Im talkin like a Kevin McHale type
white dude. Dont get me wrong Kevin is cool & all
but his hook shot was like watching an armpit. Yeah
an armpit. I be lookin at the tv screen like why they got
me watchin this armpit of a hook shot right now? Ever
wonder what the NBA would be like if we never

joined? I mean say we progressed everywhere else except
sports. You know how unpopular sports would be?
Cause they cant unsee when we play. Man they care
about our deepest fears when we out there. I suppose
thats why these pro ball players be gettin etiquette
training. So no one gets too sugary off the court. You
know what people hate worse than Black people? Black
people who act like Black people. You ever laugh real
loud in public? Shoot. Folks act like you just coughed
in their food. Boy they get so upset. So you gotta learn
to laugh like you tellin a secret. Gotta have a secret laugh.
Imagine that. Imagine the jobs we would have if
we walked around knowin bout this secret laugh. But
the problem really be these coaches man. Got this slave
master mentality. They got these grubby rough fingers
made for grabbin players right below the throat. Low
enough to scare ya into thinkin you coulda been choked.
You know my coach grabbed me once? So I held my neck
up to the ceiling light. Blinked so fast I thought I was a movie
frame. Not sure if I was scared or numb but honestly
feels like he been holdin me ever since. Never could break him
free.

HELP DEFENSE

is a funny little term. Not common in a pick-up game with uncoached
adolescent boys, but when there is an obsession for victory, help is required.

This means the kid guarding me ain't the one who chose me. Ain't smelled
my scent all game until I am midair climbing toward the basket, facing a new

defender-boy who is 6'1" with a body shaped like a punching bag. Actually, *midair*
does not accurately describe my ability so I will simply say I was *ungrounded*

& when one is *ungrounded* you either swat or stand still. There is no gray area.
The new defender-boy does neither, backswings his right elbow until he jabs my navel,

electrocutes my spine & I fall hammer-like into plywood, surprisingly without
drama. On the sidelines there are witnesses but never referees, no one brave

enough to make a call for me. The mantra remains: *no blood no foul.* Even the highest
court in the land agrees that if I ever suggested a drop was spilled, or my skin split open

after a call, they would not take my word. Blame it on my birth. Convince themselves
that pain already lived inside me.

Ashley Says Starting Your Period Feels Like a River Flowing

which in hindsight
    is disrespectful to rivers.
In fact, it feels like the last five
    seconds of peeing
after your coach warned you
    not to drink so much Gatorade.
So every month is karma
    from assuming you knew better
than elders. The first time you
    felt your pants wet in public
coulda been a prank
    prank. Like Daniel who got high
on flunking social studies
    fucked around and poured
a glass of lukewarm water
    into your seat. He'd know
better, but you are the type
    to blame other people
for acts of God. Your period
    is not a river. It is a failed
sorcerer reminding you the limits
    of black magic. I wonder
if Ashley lied about her period
    or wanted to warn me
sometimes Black girls drown
    in their own blood. Either way
I refused to rise until recess.
    Called my mother & surrendered
to the evitable. No rescue
    from my body becoming
a woman. I mourned myself
    as I cried into the phone,
ready to be saved.

BLACK RAGE I: A COLORED MUSEUM

My first fight was my last.

If you ain't got a better word
shouldn't you need a better mouth?

In the sixth grade my best friend
would have told you I knocked
that white girl out cold.
While not completely true,
I did win.
Didn't throw the first punch,
but left her back bent
like a fishing rod, before I walked
home victorious. My mouth

don't mean I'm a violent person,
but don't push me
unless you tryna lose your head.
Kidding.
I square up so pretty, though.
Gimme a mirror like Cassius,
like Morris Day
& I'ma dance on any fool
who got a poplar tree
of a tongue.

I proudly announced
these trophy fists, my clean face—
proof the white girl didn't even get
two licks on me.
My Mama said I should apologize
I said *nahhhhh*
I won.

Yo, I'm old school with it—
So Pam Grier in Original Gangstas.
So bout these hands
serving vengeance
like a charcuterie board.
Got wrath pure enough
to clean the swamp between
a white girl's lips when correctly
prompted.

    My lips had no choice
    but to openly pout
    when I was asked to change shirts
    & get into the car.
    We drove to the grassy field
    where the girl & her disheveled tank top
    had not wandered far from.

Please believe, if my people were
the vicious kind, er'body would be
a memory. We cant even kill
our own rage.

    When I approached her, the white
    girl, I swear, the Blackest thing
    I ever done was uncurl my fist
    & straighten my spine
    while my mother hovered above me.
    I served an open-mouth apology
    like a sinner with counterfeit
    remorse— maybe I believed,
    one day, this would save me.

—for that, I truly am
sorry.

_____ & BASKETBALL

One week after _Love & Basketball_ premiered, I attended my first middle
school dance. Before then, a newly formed WNBA was often synonymous
with the word ____ when used in casual conversation. The first time I was called
____ was after jumping into a swimming pool with baggy Nike swim trunks.
A boy yelled ____ with teeth grinned shut, the sun hid behind the sharp _k_,
& water, cold enough for me to drown, freezing. The film made soft-pitched
efforts to ensure Monica was not a ____ like I'd always known myself
to be. I arrived at the dance wearing a gingerbread sleeveless jumpsuit recycled
from my 6th grade graduation, a compromise with my mother. In exchange,
my hair remained braided, a low-hung ponytail. This is why they thought
we were similar, I suppose. Monica, in the scene before prom, sat between
her sister's knees. Each scalp comb-through, a winced whupping until her stubborn
hair bloomed into a mane, flipped & curled to her mother's approval. Monica wore
a bandage-tight dress & announced her sculpted quads as new characters.
The boys swooned & bent unripe knees to have a good look at the not ____ woman
she spent the entire day becoming. Her date, a college student who was unremarkable
yet handsome enough for her to seem ungrateful when her eyes vibrated toward
her true love interest. By the end of the night I, too, had been asked to dance
by a light-skinned boy with lint in his hair. He wore black overalls & a wrinkled
white t-shirt. African Musk cologne dangled from his neck, yet did not disguise
the fact he probably hadn't showered after gym. Still, I pretended this gesture
was manufactured for the ____ in me, & despite____-ish longing I reached
for his right hand, meticulous & adorned as any romantic comedy. Our clumsy
bodies collided in a slow dance to Maxwell's moans while our arms mimicked
cover art of Monica & Quincy balancing a basketball above their shoulders. Except
our lips didn't touch. Except I flinched & no one noticed. Across the room,
an autumn-haired girl named Vanessa waved the most delicate hello, though
I could have been mistaken. In my ____ mind, our eyes met beyond the declining
falsetto while her chin hung over her boyfriend's shoulder. Everything a young ____
could ask of pleasure.

FACEGUARD

type of defense is where you gotta wrestle for an empty hip,

>full-court press & knuckle clench
>a jersey like you are hiding a handful
>of jelly beans— *your nose should be starin*
>*at a chin hair.*

>The trick to beating a faceguard press
>is to plant one foot between the opponent's
>legs until half your body weight kneads
>into their chest, then sprint the opposite
>direction &— just like that— you break free.

Some girls knew this. Others just cried.

>Thought we was too close to their mouths. Thought
>we was lesbian hoodlums without the decency
>to play zone. Thought we was robbin folks
>of their right to pass the ball. Thought we
>was crotch-grabbin our shorts, smilin with corroded

>copper in our grillz. Thought we was Sticky Fingaz
>at the Source Awards. One time, instead of dribbling
>a white girl yelled for help & when the referee
>rescued her

I fouled out.

A Litany of Things That Are (Not) My Business

Asia rubs the grain of the ball way too much before she releases,
wasting a whole half second off the shot clock.

That's why her jumper got an awkward spiral
going the opposite direction of her follow through.

                                        But that ain't none of my business

until someone sets their eyes crooked enough to confuse
her game stats with mine— which is why I suppose we never been

more than cordial. Sure, we both lean with our walk & let our
gym shorts fall to our shins, but that don't make us *fam*.

                                        & I ain't one to gossip, but

her girlfriend be biting those fingernails into submission, hoping
folks don't catch the rhythm of Asia's whispering rage, or the newly formed

bruise below the elbow. Asia denying the word *girlfriend*, but we all seen
ol' girl's bangs splayed into Asia's lap while splitting sandwiches

with too much mustard during lunch hour. Figure that day
is when Asia demanded everyone call them *best friends*.

                                        That ain't none of my business, but

if I were in the same position, I guess I'd need to prove
I wasn't a lesbian to no one in particular.

Which explains why she walking around tongue-kissing
that random white boy who flosses baby blue puff-coats

& porcupine slicks his hair to prayer like he auditioning
to be the fifth member of 98 Degrees.   ·

                                        & I ain't one to gossip, but

Asia's girlfriend would stand parallel to them humping
against the lockers & wait patiently until they finished.

& they might've been the first *best friends*
we'd seen, so we all left Asia's girl alone cause

                                                            it ain't our business

to repair the wreckage of a secret relationship. When folks
say Asia & I look alike, all I hear is *yall just wanna be like*

yo daddies— even though we wouldn't even share the same shade if she camped
on the sun & her daddy ain't shit & honestly the inside of our palms

be rivals most days. So when coach wanna put her in the starting
lineup, I think about the girlfriend's newly decorated forearm,

the raised backhand I peeped the week before & how this ain't the brand
of violence the wig-swapping eleven o'clock news reporter prepared us for

& who could I think to call when the closeted, girlfriend-less girl cries
for help? & I guess I come from a school of: when one girl devastates

another, both are at fault by choosing each other in the first place & I suppose
I feared being outed or rather, called my real name before this cheap-ass world

was ready to hear it & I'm bettin Asia could smell the *stud* in me. So she thinkin
I want her girl & I be thinkin hell nah I just want you to stop pretendin

pretendin yo jumpshot ain't some *half-eaten spoiled fruit pie in the bottom of the waste pile*
& I guess that's why I play defense on her with my eyes first, teeth into bone

type of guarding, to let her know she ain't the kin I wanna inherit nothin from
so don't even think about rubbin that weak-ass shit off on me.

Sweeter Than a Swisher

Everybody wants to be a Black girl until the last fingertip
of relaxer is pressed into the brain, which means the burn,
by now, is so roused a rattail comb can sing through your scalp
without static & no one gives consolation prizes to whomever
can hold these chemicals the longest before the rinse, cause if they did
you would be sure to collect your winnings. But, at the shop

you gotta fix your face, or at least stop acting
like you got someplace better to be, even if the boxed
TV mounted in the corner ceiling is repeating
the same movie & you arrived while *The Young & The Restless*
is still on rotation but that's okay, cause you love when Munirah
talks at the screen or repeats a saucy line before cackling. By evening,

every seat in the shop is occupied with a woman (or her purse) breathing
heavy from the stress of rush-hour traffic, including your mother
who convinced Munirah to add extra curls just for this occasion
& guarantees you won't sweat it out before your senior photos
tomorrow & though Munirah loves to argue with your mother about
how that ain't the type of girl you seem to be, she obliges,

holds a hot iron close like a whisper & flips the tips into capital
J's & now your hair looks like it pays the cable bill & neck rolls
R&B songs out a second-floor window about how *she don't need
no man*. When your mama is happy with the result you decide
sometimes her joy is worth being someone else for.
Her satisfaction multiplies on car ride home while fixing

loose strands like crooked silverware— as if she can finally see
the resemblance. She calls your Auntie Robbin & Auntie Yasmin
& the rest of your friends' mamas & asks to stop by each home
& she promises you Wendy's if you just get out of the car & stretch
your cheeks to supply a grin. Give them a cupped wave— spin around
like you ain't still got basketball shorts on because tonight is all about the hair.

Oh the hair. This Black girl magic trick is old as vaseline.
Proof, there must still be a woman inside.

BANGERS

My Auntie bought panties
for my high school graduation—
a gift—
bubble gum
cheap lace,
not quite thong,
but adjacent,
like first cousin,
panties.

To not disappoint
I tried them on.

Cuuuuute,
was the verdict.
Murder
Was the Case
bops
in my head.

This a banger—
my body
a drive-by,
roll-up,
so dishonest
wannabe
Vivica,
yet so much
Suge Knight
swells this neckline.

I say
thank you

like I walked onstage
to perform
my acceptance speech.

Gawd look at all yo trophies just sittin there like cold
pancakes. Bet they heavy. Ever use too much flour in
your batter? Got em soundin like Flintstones when you
flip over? Tastin like maple clay? Sweet aint the same
as good ya know. Im just sayin some things dont
need to stick around just cause they was made. I get
why you keepin your trophies though. Sometime we gotta
get high off them memories. I remember my mama
used to hold on to these decorated plates she been
draggin around since childhood. It wasnt fine china or
nothin fancy like that. Just three or four white & blue
trimmed plates we couldnt eat off. Id be so mad like
aint that the whole purpose of havin em? To eat? After
some years she tucked em away in a closet to keep em
from collectin dust. When she got older I cleaned the house
& finally thought to ask about the damn plates & she
mentioned this neighbor. Ms Mary I think her name
was. Yeah lets go with that. Thats who passed them down
to her. Man when she spoke about Ms Mary youd swear
she was still six years old in Biloxi Mississippi. Tellin you
aint nothin more frightening than a full grown up
becoming a child on accident. Yeah I guess Ms Mary
helped out a lot around the house when she was young. Fixed
her hair taught some songs & passed down a few recipes.
I suppose everybody need a Ms Mary to remember. Boys
specially if ya ask me. Just kinda strange to keep those
plates though. Dont ya think? But I get it. Sometimes
you just need a break from who you are. Thats what I be
thinkin when folks be bruised with nostalgia. I be like
oh you just wanted to get high. You just needed to forget
about right now for a second. Ha! Cant be mad at it
except when they become hoarders. You cant keep it all.
Sometimes you gotta just live expectin to forget. Shoot
I bet you cant even tell which trophy belongs to which team
huh? How old were you? Who was there? What shoes
were you wearing? Man when my team won the conference
back in the day we didnt get no individual awards. We shared
a big ol human sized trophy. Half of Shaqs body. Heavy
as a tombstone. Held it above our shoulders. Posed

with it under me like it was my third leg. Shoot
got a photo somewhere in this house & I bet I can tell you
erbody on the roster. Who their siblings are. The girl
they was datin at the time. But if you really fixed on seein
that trophy ya could probably find it behind some locked glass
in the school hallway bein as useless as month old bread.
Thats why I always say ya better keep growin young. The
actual trophy never matters young buck. Question is can
you remember? Try this. Give a lil girl all yo good plates
& see how long she keep em. Thats the game.

PEDAGOGY
OR; INSTEAD OF LEARNING ABOUT SEX IN YOUR HEALTH EDUCATION CLASS

Go ahead & find an older lesbian

or rather someone aged enough to remember,
yet care less about Ellen DeGeneres coming out
in 1997. Promise her top shelf dark liquor

or a fanny pack of pre-rolled joints
or a sincere compliment

about her skin-care regimen
in exchange for a story or two about why she never
washed her mouth with the word *queer*.

& after she explains how that language is more
gentrified than a waitlisted Sunday morning brunch line,
ask her how to woo.

& if you are humble enough to respect her story
ain't the same as yours, she will only tell you what is urgent
& even if she doesn't, she is still proof you exist, so

be sure to learn her name.

MUSIC OF MY MIND: A LIP SYNC VANGUARD

Sometimes I pretend to sing

like an eight-year-old

who professes to know how to Motown 25 moonwalk

by way of cotton ankle socks on a cold linoleum floor,

meaning I'm the most wholesome phony out here.

Back in the day my Grammy would elect me

& my cousins as a show choir right before the congregation's

eyes & we'd unveil a tune we had only just learned an hour prior

when our bodies were stacked sweaty in a station wagon

on the way to morning service—

only a trained eye would dare question my allegiance to God cause I swear

God there was no noise released from these lips,

only an imitation of worship.

I was that kid

who called myself a sinner first,

knew the most rotten words to name myself,

became adept in never sharing

what could burden or save

me. All these years, love was rehearsed

& my silence required a larger stage. My dear,

you will never understand the music of my mind,

so many songs inside of me

you will never hear.

To all the straight girls I have loved before who all seem to write in cursive
to the curses to heart dotted i's to origami letters you pull to pushing
the pen to promise always yet never to the friendship first to the home-cooked
hugs low & slow in the crevice of a locker room to the hips in the Tommy Girl
jeans to the toothbrush comb to the baby hair bangin to the arched bangs
to the supervised sleepover to the hot breath beneath the covers to the *I don't*
usually but umm & *We can't again but umm* to the *bang* shotgun of a public eye
to the fly on the wall to the chokehold of shame to the laugh wicked whisper
wildly to the lion's mouth to the unhinged parents to the pariah to the bible
study the blasphemy the belief in nothing outside of lust & still lingering
& lingerie to *lucky him* to the bloody hymns to the gospel of desire to the local
radio station to the coded dedication to the olive juice to the one-four-three
to the *just think of me as the pages in your diary* to the one tune we agreed
would be ours & ours only & eventually everyone's *Always & Forever.*

If you don't like rhythm & blues
the bigot in you might be the size of a South Carolina

Cracker Barrel— just sayin— but who knows
why one repels themselves from the delicate

timbre of Stevie's harmonica if they indeed
have love resting wholly on their hearts.

My college roommate was all Metallica & chairless
concerts with black eyeliner. She was all Linkin Park

& home-cut jean jackets & she was all like *why*
every song from your music gotta sound the same,

Black girl?

Well she didn't say *Black girl* but she said *your*
music like a dry biscuit would say *your people.*

I treated it as such & responded with the only
comeback my daddy ever taught me

So? What about your face?

If you don't like rhythm & blues
perhaps you just ain't never wanted nothin

sweet in the first place, nobody worth extending a song
three minutes for, or maybe ain't used to seeing us beg

for nothin outside of our self-respect. Ain't too proud
to lay on concrete for a whole b-side if it means we live

to dance with lovers who pour sugar in our ankles.
If you don't like rhythm & blues you don't love

me or the child I am eternally becoming
who crawls curling into her own lap, drifting

open-lipped bouncing love off the tongue like grown
folks like ancestors like all the medicine we ever needed

until all I see is Black.

It wasn't no real first kiss or nothin cuz we didn't use tongue
but it was a sexual healing type of 808 snare into a whisper
of *wake up wake up wake up* when our mouths bumped
maybe accidentally cuz of the circumstance & I don't care
what nobody say, *Chevys* ain't a real date but *Chevys on the River* go hard
enough on an August night that I deserved a lil frenchery
& I didn't push my luck cuz what's important is she wasn't wearin
her work scrub so maybe that mean she rushed home after
or intended to be sexy then decided to scale it back with this cropped
polo shirt. I bought a thirty dollar ring from Walmart cuz my best friend
say I should be prepared & stop writing her poems named after Stevie tracks
cuz what if she pulls em out of a drawer eight years from now? & what song
screams *I'm leaving for college next week & you got a girl, but here's a promise ring?*
Wear it til we decide what to call this soundtrack or til yo finger turn jealous.

I swear Stevie did a cover of *I'm the One Who Loves You* I been practicin
in the mirror for at least a decade & Stevie beg like the good man
I'm tryna be or the type that knows a mouth is the best instrument
when the feels be reciprocal. So yeah, we kiss after dinner on a cloudless night.
There's this mariachi band that ain't takin no breaks & I'ma call
them The Funk Brothers for now cuz this trumpet tellin me how to hold
her hips & this kid next to us talkin bout this river look like an ocean
so maybe erbody here is dumb or maybe we on an island
with Motown in our eyes & some big ass bottom lips smearin
Carmex on each other just to avoid callin it quits, but this breeze
is too perfect for words & what song exudes *my first date was our last date*
& I swear Texas ain't that far & yes I'm already packed but also been preparin
for us my whole life except for a lil more tongue to be honest.
It's complicated to know exactly & everything you want for a moment.

To Hear Her Tell It

If you ask me, I was acting brand new. Meaning, I walked like I had sex
& required everyone to smell it on me.

No longer a broken-wrist-watch-of-a-girl who dressed like her brother.
Instead, I strut to an imaginary soundtrack from an era my new flat top

would cherish. My wardrobe, brimming with slim-cut button downs, squared
evenly around my shoulders. My boots, an upgrade from the karate shoes

acquired in high school. I must admit, my memories are my least stable
friendships, but I do recall feeling buoyant for a moment in time while returning

home for the holidays until entering the local grocery store. My stride, interrupted
by my name shouted from the produce aisle, on repeat, like I was a lost pre-teen

at a carnival. The woman responsible, I recognized. She worked in the front
office of my elementary school & *then* my middle school & *also* my high school.

Her face, salt-colored with foundation. Hair, barely pulled back & stray bangs
waving for attention. After a hearty embrace, I noticed her wrinkles looked drawn,

like each memory she carries, left a stain on the edge of her smile.
After greeting me, she began remembering, out loud— & for no apparent

reason— the first day I started my period. & by the way she told it, you could
swear she was recounting the March on Washington.

This unearned pride, this thorned witness, this fixation on how I began.

So I stared into the rifts around her lips, & graciously listened to her story
of my blood— forgetting who I came there hoping to become.

When you really think about it. Erbody is losing at halftime.

—Nash

Woo

Tasha say she discovered me. After practice
she would follow me into the parking lot

behind the gym, tug
my mesh jersey toward her waist,

lift a penciled brow, ask
to be cupped with both hands

inside her back pockets. Tasha say
she never been with a woman

before. Say she had dreams once or twice
in high school, but never considered

touch til now. Say she feel herself wet
in class sometimes. Gotta excuse herself

from the dinner table. Gotta tell her Auntie
how we suddenly became good friends.

Tasha say she got a boyfriend but
he don't take classes around here.

Tasha say she would break up with him
soon, or now, or yesterday if I went

down on her & so I do. & I think I said
I loved her then. & after, she turned

over, bare back facing the wall outlet
to check if he messaged her. Tasha say

she saved though I ain't known her to say grace
over no meals. Tasha say *her* Jesus must be the reason

she kept ol' boy around so long. Say it only makes sense
to bring him home this holiday. Tasha say

I should move on. Tasha changes her mind
while slurring the lyrics to a Freddie Jackson track.

Tasha grips my cheeks & kisses me
under a half-eaten moon. Tasha calls

from a blocked number. Tasha sings a lullaby
of an apology into my voicemail. Tasha

gossips to her teammate about how she gonna
meet my parents. Tasha memorizes my class

schedule. Tasha waits outside of the science
building. Tasha is pregnant. Tasha does not

tell me for five months. & I think I said
I loved her then. I think *I will raise*

a child with a woman who will choose me
sometimes. Tasha say I was her blessing

lil man gotta have a real daddy tho.

Say she drivin seventeen hours south next week
to meet him in Jacksonville. Tasha say the sun

is a snitch, makin us too public for her ideal goodbye.
Thought folks in the gymnasium parking lot

may get the wrong idea. Tasha holds both arms
above my shoulders & barely grazes my skin

before she drives off. Tasha say sorry
she don't be callin often. Sends a photo

of her healthy baby boy. I fool myself
thinkin his smile looks like mine.

—

Ms. Peggy spit her baby hair back held flat split tongue

black eyes rolled sky I pause spine stiff she sniff

no air just shade tells me *hat off* I say *okay okay* she say

Why you lookin like you rob a bank huh? All gawk inhale

gurl what's your bra size? XL growth spurt flirt posture

upright imposter skin-tight don't fit skin might fly like

popped grease popped neck sit still girl check that fat thick

lip puff put some pearls round yo neck *Ooh get em!*

If you got the knees bend em go head party hop this city

you been pretty since 1920 stroll like a bass drum kicked back

white & blue kick back pristine syntax *sho nuff* roll up

to the banquet blouse shirt nurse skirt pantyhose all holes

holy shackle sweet tabernacle

Why you wear foundation if you don't know how to do it?

Why you got that booty if you don't know how to use it?

Two steppin like you got some lava in yo cup

girl we be face down ass up cuz that's the way we like to—

& girl you looked so cute back when yo mama picked yo clothes

I said *I didn't ask no questions* I'd just hold my head & pose.

INITIATION
Club Colours, 18+ Lesbian Nightclub, Richmond VA, circa 2006

I never understood the craze over Tootsie Pops. Dyed sugar & paper wrap flavoring
 disintegrating into pretend chocolate. But every stud-dom-butch girl

in this joint got an empty lollipop swab hangin out the edge of their mouth
 like a toothpick, except me. Despite the hour I spent ironing with razor

sharp starch, all sore thumbs point to my tilted pinstripe fedora & almost matching
 button up I borrowed (stole) from my brother's closet. I fit in

because I sprayed a semester's worth of DKNY Be Delicious onto my shirt pocket.
 I stand out because my tan Lugz are pretending to be Timberland boots.

Virginia is indeed the South because the bouncer refuses to lower their stadium cup
 of sweet tea while checking our IDs. From the corridor, a tornado of smoke

stains our shirts before circling each PA speaker generously honoring Lil Scrappy's
 entire catalog of music. The teammates I came with straight up look like

Lil Bow Wow apprentices. Their white headbands are billboards covering
 their line up push-backs. Each pair of Air Force 1's make them appear

as if they don't have ankles but match their oversized tees, draped in mall kiosk
 gold. After the second security check, they disperse like it is Black

Friday. Baby oil their confidence into the hips of nameless women before saying
 hello. If it were dawn, this place could pass for a bodega, confined

like a sweat & slicked sugar shack where every crotch lives to graze every booty
 in this building. I steal an unused wall & suck ice cubes from a water cup

Peptalking my will to dance until my head ticks noticeably against the song's measure.
 Then panic-slide my root foot to the other on-beat, all Temptations-like.

until I hear my teammate shout from two grind positions away *Who you think*
 you is? Usher? So I chill, like *you right.* Cross my arms like a middle school

Chaperone. Like I am letting the children bump bootys against school wishes,
 until I catch a beat drop & this woman with more bare legs than any

other body part takes notice. I must assume she is tipsy cause she is holding
 a half-empty plastic cup of blue hurricane (club sanctioned jungle juice)

& though she has been switching dance partners all night, I am honored
    to be seen. She squints before pinching my stomach

with rhinestone sapphire nails, she backs me into another's back & now I gotta
    apologize to the room for the domino effect of spilled liquor.

Make a plan to hold a trained defensive stance because I am too sober
    to fall. End up wrapping my right arm around her waist, so soft

I'm sure it tickled. I don't surrender. Instead, I glue my tongue to the corner
    of my mouth like the other stud-dom-butches around me.

Like MJ head above the rim—but probably looked like I was catching snowflakes
    out the side of my mouth. Sure, I naturally dance on my tippy toes

but this cannot be the moment I'm exposed for my sin— so I pretend
    like I'm one of the pledges I saw at last week's probate who almost lost

his balance while eagle-posting on one foot. Cement my ankles & clutch
    what is left of her drunken generosity until this song blends

into another. She walks away to find another dance partner when an older
    stud-dom-butch abandons her spot at the bar to dap me

with a calloused hand & an empty lollipop swab hanging from her lip.
    Though I was unclear as to what she mumbled, she added *fam*.

LESSONS ON BEING BALD-HEADED

Let us celebrate my cousin's locs. Decades young & draped— decorated down
her back if she so chooses. But sometimes an updo, loose bun or a common
hair tie, tied up with her own damn hair. Trust, growth is no easy feat.

If this were a kitchen, our hair type would be a slow cooker on warm.
Hell, by the time I turned twenty-two, the leaves that blossomed
from my scalp hardly reached the top of my shoulders.

That's why folk think we be emptied women, *gon' mad gals*, say our souls
be bankrupt when we announce *everything must go* & chop this forest down
to brush then pose, unbothered— without lamenting our loss. The first time

I was called *sir* without correction was at a 7-Eleven, hours after a barber raked
the last of my hair clippings into a trashcan. While shopping, the cashier noticed
my new fade & AAU molded shoulders, & perhaps decided his fear was superior

to my future— convinced I stole a sixty-cent pack of Rolos, though I purchased
other items. Despite myself, I agree to empty my pockets & scratched this fresh scalp
in confusion before he reached underneath the counter, demanded I lower my hands

& dialed 911.

When the Officer Asks Me to Get Out of the Vehicle, *I*

1. Spit
   a. Into my throat
   b. Onto his forehead
   c. Toward the cement
      i. Stained my front teeth
      ii. An unforgiving shade of fear
      iii. To mark the right spot
         1. Before finding words
         2. To soil my history
         3. Like this is worth falling for
            a. Spare me
            b. Take it
            c. Right there

2. Plead
   a. To God
   b. To the waving baton
   c. To the empty parking lot
      i. Can I get a witness
      ii. Who made you this brave
      iii. Am I dust to you
         1. I want to believe in you
         2. Find belonging in someone else's hands
         3. No one will be the same
            a. After this
            b. Man, listen
            c. I want to be saved

3. Sing
    a. We Shall Overcome
    b. Dancing In The Streets
    c. Waiting to Exhale
        i. Deep in my heart, I do believe
        ii. All we need is music, sweet music
        iii. This Is How It Works
            1. Truth will make us free
            2. The time is right
            3. Not Gon' Cry
                a. We are not afraid today
                b. Are you ready for a brand new beat?
                c. It Hurts Like Hell

BLACK RAGE II: FOREWARNING

I briefly dated a Jamaican woman who said if I pissed her off
she would pour hot oil in my ear while I was sleeping. The bright side

of becoming feverishly terrified of this woman was her unyielding
honesty (we never slept in the same bed after an argument).

If you've ever caught hold of a hood fight you'd know, before the first punch
chews into a raw bone, there is always a clear warning— verbal caution.

If you _____, I will_____.

If you touch me without permission, I will aim low & tender.
If you use that word one more time, I will knock it back into your tonsils.
If you don't respect me, I will emotionally burn this motha fucka down like I ain't
need no roof.

& just like a railroad advance warning sign,
it ain't personal.
Should have seen it coming.

My Neighbor Nash Say, Part III

Did you know the first time I met my wife,
I was coming to school in the same jeans
erday? No lie. Probably looked as raggedy
as a wet cat. Been with her since. Never
heard a single complaint about my attire
neither. Shit. I wish my audacity on the world
sometimes. I guess folks just scared
nowadays bout what someone might whisper
bout you under they breath. Aye look
at me when I say this. You know
what your problem is? You worried bout
the wrong shit. I mean you gotta remember
to live cuz a lifetime aint forever.
Just sayin. I got friends who spent years
talkin themselves out of a good time.
You ever been to a party or a bar
& just ruined your own fun?
Just by havin a conversation with
yourself? Shoot might as well drink
Ripple. Im just sayin. Personally. If I
wasnt tryna to have fun thats what Id do.
Id drink Ripple. Theres this phrase
my cousin Tony always told me. He said
the best musicians make some of the worst
music. For example who yo favorite?
Classic. Okay well Stevie Wonder
had an awful album about plants
or some shit. I remember the day
that mess came out. Shoot. I really
dont know which drug the govment
coulda planted to make someone create
an album like that. But at the end
of the day he is still Stevie. Just sayin.
You gotta start makin some of your worst
music now kid. Let that sink in.
I honestly might be the only cat in town
talkin hot trash about Stevie
Wonder right now. I figure thats good
odds for him. Ill gladly admit that I cant

do what he does. Stevie plays over fifteen
instruments. Ever notice the only folk
laughin at you are ones who dont do
what you can? I figure I earned this life
though. Woke up every mornin at 4am
just to be at work by 7am just to be home
by 10pm. Did that for thirty somethin years
kid. So you better believe Im the best
at what I do. Da goat. Ill shout that
in a Groucho Marx lookin white guys
ear any day. I mean aint that
what time is for? To count down
the days til you can call yourself the best?
Thats why Im retired. Shit all Im sayin
is you gotta learn how to play the game
like it cant belong to no one else.
I see you hesitatin before you shoot.
Slidin yo tongue into a statue of fear
like you waitin on folks to abandon you.
I always go back to that story bout my wife
cause you cant stop livin waitin for someone
to love you. Nobody want you til you get
just a lil more greedy kid. Just sayin
as long as you know the value of the assist
you cant ever be selfish.

LESSONS ON BEING TENDERHEADED

I.

You know when you gettin braided up by a woman who aint really
yo kin? But friendly enough wit yo mama to smack the back
of your head wit her comb cause you movin too much? Or maybe
she figures you just gon put these eighty or ninety micro-braids she done
spent a whole half-day weavin together into a ponytail anyhow? So here
she go damn near deadlifting each crop of your scalp pullin strands
of greased hair all Luke Cage-like like, are you a superhero lady?
Are your fingers made of brass metal? & you feel the skin of your forehead
forklift itself an inch higher than what you thought humanly possible?
& you don't cry? Because you can't cry? Because being tenderheaded
is worse than being disobedient?

II.

Because I have never screamed full octave, I pay close attention
to the church soloist. A fresh perm leaning her neck sideways
into the choir's call— her response, a sharp undeciphered wail
drying everyone's face still. Not many achieve this on command.
Black girls rot themselves to soil learning to scream on key.
For this reason, I have mastered lip-syncing woes into a bathroom
mirror. The wide-eyed howl. My once white teeth circle each syllable.
The safety of moans buried inside of me. My partner knows this trick—
counts the seconds my chest refuses to move, hushes my smallest screams
before urging me to breathe. True, I have always been all tantrum,
no choir. Oh, how I wish I could burst open robeless, haywire, thorned
without consequence. Once, my grandmother carelessly rested her hot comb
against my soft flesh. Crisped my ear to burnt toast. Out fled an ailing,
full-bellied, Black vaudeville roar turned cackle. Hearty enough to trick
my damn self from tears.

III.

Oh, us tenderheads—
how we normalize sacrifice,
cause *Don't nobody want to hear you*
fester, child. Sputter, holler, or scoop
your bottom lip. Unless you sound like Aretha.
Unless you dead. Is you dead?
Thought so.

IV.

When I oblige the comb's orders, I uncoil my back.
Count to fifteen. Clench my booty. Stab my veined forearm
with freshly bloomed nails. Softly hiss between my teeth. Curse
these eyes until they thirst. I know how to follow instructions
dammit. Never been the type to ask for a raise— or kiss my partner
in front of family. Willing to wait until the next layover to find
a single-stall bathroom. How much has died to make me this strong?

V.

Even now, on my most unkempt days, when the barber plays gently
with my matted scalp, I practically boast when I assure him
I can take it. *I aint tenderheaded no more.* Meaning, you can now lift
a fine-toothed comb from root to end without a flinch.
The barber does not know enough of what I have lived through to care.
He nicks the back of my neck. Gossips into a warm spit over my head.
Styles a cut I never asked for. My torso remains still as a gravestone—
Black women taught me well. I thank him for his services. Wipe
the blood from the back of my neck. Remember to leave a tip.

ETIQUETTE

Kind of like a steel-brimmed
& armored medieval knight
who removes their helmet as
a gesture of obedience to their king,

I lift my snapback & carry it
below my right hip before entering
the women's restroom to reassure
those who are concerned

I am not a threat.

ANKLE WEIGHTS

Jump like no bone could ever scatter to dust
or grieve in silence. Like your knees could
survive the soft heat of a ratchet bullet. See how
fear & gravity eat at the same table?

You know there was no such thing as prayer
until we imagined we could touch
the sky? To shed your blues, you gotta wear
sorrow like a wool scarf. Start with two
pounds. Then, five. Then, ten. Then, none.

Then, see? How your legs no longer feel
like somebody owns them? Like a thicket
of autumn air? Like a shackle stubborn to latch
the ankle? You, too slippery to hold. You, heavy-headed,

crown pose enamored by this new shadow.
When niggas jump, you finally enunciate each syllable
around their name. When niggas jump, you mistake
them as Gods in a moonlit park. They say,
if you choose all of this weight you might break

yourself. Strain a tendon. Snap your confidence
in half for a spell. If you choose to soar wingless,
you may scratch your cheek on this good earth
when you land, or learn what's capable of catching
you.

QUEER DIVORCE
BUT NOT REALLY CAUSE WE WERE JUST DATING

In the not quite divorce settlement
my ex calls dibs on the $1800 sectional sofa,
charcoal grey & long enough for separate
sleeping arrangements— we bought it a week after
the fight our therapist could not repair & when
the sales associate offered us the protection plan
she leaned her head on my shoulder & asked
are you certain we're ready for this?

//

My neighbor's son & his cabbage-patch-stretched
-cheeks statues himself outside of the trash bag
packed apartment before waving hello, which was also
goodbye, & I gesture back like I've just boarded
a departing ship.

//

We share keys to the nearest storage locker,
assume we can revisit split purchases when
the initial shock begins to thaw.
The griddle, the ottoman, the foam mattress—
there is no intentional planning, just time.
My cousin's guest room precedes the new lease.
The new lease precedes the Tempurpedic.
Tempurpedic precedes actual sleep.
Sleep is a luxury for the HGTV 'round here,
for the fixer-upper Him & Hers
move-in ready fresh-brewed-dark-roast
-on-master-bedroom-balcony 'round here.
No queer role models 'round here.
Only ancestors & Sundance.

//

The local bartenders know the correct spelling
of my first name, the way my mama named me
with an accent between the *a* & the *e*.
I've grown accustomed to Mezcal & bitter
fruit— only wake when it is required of me,
laugh until I spit leftovers into the mirror,
sleep open-mouthed, purchase noise cancellation
headphones to avoid hearing myself breathe.
Look for sugar wherever I can find it, until
I find less joy in common sweetness & my ankles
weaken & I practice staring at my pores in a
clean mirror. Each divot, both temporary
& forever.

//

Awe quit ya mopin,
only fools wait on apologies.
Look at ya lookin like
an ashy ankle,
a bottom lip of vaseline,
a warm ginger ale type.
You so sad, when you look in the mirror
you make yourself hiccup.
You soggy & I think you like being soggy.
Go brush yo teeth a lil harder.
Taste some real blood.

//

If you love me, don't ask why we aren't together,
but also assume I want to be asked.
If you liked us together, keep it to yourself.
Don't nobody bring me no bad news
Tell 'em I'm allergic to water & this depression
be vast as the Sahara at dusk.
Do you really want to know
how I'm doing? You sure?
Knew you was lyin.
A friend who has met her twice
says he misses our relationship
& I reply *I'm sorry for your loss, bruh.*

//

Her friends were never your friends.
Her family, never your kin.
You wince whenever her name crawls
into the same sentence as yours.
Trust no one.
The key in-between fist type.
Count every exhale type.
Even a full moon can be lying, too,
you know? You ever seen something
so reliable be good to you?

//

My brother's wedding travel was already arranged
so we make a plan to be cordial, share
a queen-size bed just for the weekend,
& dance to distract the room from asking why
we're not living together.
There are still trash-bags to empty.
Cable receipts to settle.
Still one more wedding next month.
But the DJ sneaks a pinch of Frankie Beverly
into our liquor & we allow this room to imagine
our bones are so limber we must be ungrieved.

//

No one knows where my tears are
held hostage.
Each mourning wants
someone to blame.
I am too much Black
man to plead innocence.
Her biggest flex is that her cry
echoes loud & inevitable.
When everyone sprints
to console the tantrummed throat,
show them your desert.
How you swallowed the sand
to hold it all in.

//

The homies say we petty dykes,
we emotional thieves who stick
around til the floor ache.
Maybe the only lesbians
going to hell are the ones
who cannot communicate
how they need to be loved
after all these years
unconsoled. Maybe healing
begins when you stop
apologizing to the wrong
people. Maybe love
is like entering a showroom
with plush furniture no honest
worker could reasonably afford.
& I bet they were talking
about how we each ended up
with half of a couch, my half
sitting in my bedroom
like punishment.

//

To think, I offered her the whole thing
& it didn't fit.

ODE TO MY RIPPED PANTS

The third ones this year. Clean down the crotch & a patch
of my boxers be a moon er'body wanna gaze at.

            Come child
       & let me tell you the story about my precision.
    How you could've sworn I soared from free-throw line,
           hurdled a splintered fence,
         spread-eagled atop jeep wranglers.
     No skin lost, nor debris feathering to the ground.
            My body so industrial
         it outlasts everything around me.

O this elastic flesh.
My stretch marks actin a damn fool. These grooves
of malt liquor skin lookin like a galaxy made of soil. I marvel
at how I blemished this body to perfection. The time
it takes to scar the skin so good it refuses
to heal.

            O healing; or
      the last time I took my pants to a seamstress.
       How her eyes wandered below my waist
    before explaining this was nothing she could possibly
   repair. I forget how heavy I am sometimes. Might as well
        be blues. Might as well be anvil dropping from
   a fixed sky. I forget how taxing it becomes, waiting for others
              to lift me.

I ripped my pants
so I will buy another pair, the size of my freshest
wounds. Nothing died. In fact, there is glory
somewhere here, Black girl.

        Remember in middle school?
    When one of your microbraids fell to the sidewalk?
   & how folks wanted so badly for you to be ashamed
      for leaving a piece of yourself right there
         for everyone to see?

ODE TO MY MANSPREAD

These ungripped kitchen tongs.
O, repellent shins,
a sixth love language.
Undomesticated & gorgeous
like a restless rain cloud
widening the sky.
There is nothing to blame
for the once empty seat I occupy.
No privilege smeared when my knees
point east, then west, then exhale—
like I just performed a lifetime
of labor with little compensation.
Make no mistake,

I deserve to be everywhere.

'I Am Learning to Love Myself in Pieces'

— *Jade Cho*

Even though I am not a natural point guard   I see everything.
Watchdog swiped hands,
clumsy bones, tipsy-mouthed fathers
with shards of glass between their teeth.
I called the foul before the referee.
I stole the ball before your signature move. I am sneaky
elbow defense. You prolly just realized I fouled you   fifteen years later.
Keep up!   My form was always seen as crooked
wrist   shot put hope.
However   no   one   can   outshoot me.
Not   even   Reggie.
Not   even   now.

I am bougie as shit today.
High siddity & what mothafucka?
I only drink drip coffee of my own making.
French vanilla creaming the hell outta two pound
ceramic mugs & got the nerve to add cloves too.   *Pow!*
I write in a sketchbook til the page laughs back
& I reply *Hahaha! You right!* Add my name to the end
of Thuggish Ruggish Bone & drive my 2006 Toyota Corolla
hella hella slow windows down circlin San Pablo Park. *Sucka!*
Paid rent then poured a glass of that 14.5% red wine
cuz I ain't drinkin just to be drinkin. Cooked chicken in duck fat.
Grease   popped   so   loud   neighbors
gotta   cover   their   ears   again.
Ya scared?
Ya should   *be.*

I am a fixed meal of Motown on Mondays in Oakland.
Slide on my stank sneakers.   Tuck a sweat towel   in my pocket.
Arrive when the floor is empty enough to make room
for my knees. Side-eye when the DJ plays any song
my father wouldn't recognize. Then drunken & slobbering
yell *play some Smokey. I came to hear Smokayyyyyyyyyyyy!*
Give no fucks that I didn't pay a cover. Yo I am a life
& a party so you should actually pay me. Hell yeah I robot

with a crown. Cup of Crown Royal with a crowd
shuckin round me just cuz I hit em wit one shoulder pop.   *Check it!*
Got em.   Get off me.   I can go low too,
so low,   so low
you can't see me.

Give me all your snow & I will lift
an entire city clean using only my thighs.
My muscle mass may have decreased
but my common sense is higher.
Higher   than   your   IQ.
Go ahead & try to leave me behind
when the apocalypse arrives
But ask   Coach   Hill
— my   second   wind   is   deadly.

I am fedora hat wall & New Jack City
inspired gold chain. Turmeric & clay mask
pores. My socks match the fifth color
you recognized from my shirt. More importantly,
every   thing   I   own   fits me.
My new love calls me *stunning* & I am
comfortable & I
finally
reply

thank   you.

ANDRAGOGY
OR; HOLD ME

If you hold me, let it be
like God holds the world.

Let your cheekbone graze the soil
of my chest. Slowly glide your palms

around my waist. Press your fingertips
into each splinter of skin & trust

neither of us will bleed tonight.
This is how you hold me.

> Have you ever listened
> to the heaving ribcage of a Black girl?
>
> Sounds like a sunken treasure chest.
> There's something holy about learning to swim
>
> for the sake of discovery.
> You find nothing is extinct.
>
> Blood is eternal when it surrenders to tides
> & gold is the least of her worth. Have you felt her skin?
>
> Isn't it selfless as a Sunday sunrise? Bones melting
> like lava returning to Earth's nest. Her uneven spine & bursting
>
> belly splitting the same heartbeat. You will hear
> languages she was never taught to speak
>
> or speak up to. She is pained but it is not your job
> to undo. Follow her breath as the first flicker of light.
>
> Do not assume any part of her has walked
> your earth before. Listen.

If there is ever a time to underestimate your strength,
it is when you decide to hold me.

> Have you ever lost yourself in the heaven
> of a Black girl's eyes?

It is like watching an army
of Gods carving a sunset.

& have you ever kissed the bare back
of a Black girl? It is like drinking

sugar out of a honey jar, lips tickled sweet.
Her shoulders bloom-sprouted wings

so celestial the act feels senseless,
like gravity teaching itself to stay

still. Ever felt her rage? Like a pendulum
injecting her forearms, swinging

her breath, coloring a charcoal sky.
Yes, that quickened thunderstorm you've seen

— mayhem, red-eyed temper— was never inside of her.
Can you not feel this now?

When you hold her, she is close-eyed brightness,
underground parachute, blanket-warm cotton

beneath a somersault. See? This molten-colored fury
was not inside of her, only the world trying to become her.

There is something too patient about the moon
& I never understood why we choose to sleep

when there is so much darkness to consume.
So fuel me in my unrest tonight & hold me

tight & willingly like God held the world, like rainfall
held the gossip of heaven, like the first time

you held your laughter, both hands locking your lips
& your lungs pulsing its rupture. Listen.

If there was ever a time to listen to a Black girl
it is when she tells you exactly how to hold her,

to follow every wound of flesh & spin
your palm lines underneath her scarred chin

& stay. Like there could be no light replaced
by your eyes. Stay.

This is how you hold me.

after Ernest Gibson III

WHEN I EXTEND MY KNEE & CURL MY ANKLE

it mimics a barrel of Rice Krispies submerged
in milk. An unabashed wail like I survived
several hot bullets to the left shin. I am dramatic
because I am an athlete. I am an athlete because
I love theater— love my past life of diving
skin-first, chasing a ball rolling out of bounds,
a seated gymnasium applauding my effort. But today,
I boast without merit. Beat my chest bruised
when my legs afford me the opportunity to squat
for bottom-shelf chicken broth without strain.
Meanwhile, neighborhood children sprint uphill
with gentle ease & my stank attitude salts the sidewalks.
Don't that hurt? I want to interrupt their cocky-ass stride.
Deliver the gospel of fractured joints. My crooked cane
of a pinky. How I refuse to ice because I am a gangsta
at heart & gangstas hate feeling cold. I want to whisper
into their souls *nothing is forever.* I want to envision
them as full-faced adults who awake to lower back
pain. Instead, I pray their knees remain limber
& they never retire from a job they never wanted
in the first place. Walk home to nurse my shins in honor
of their future heartbreak.

Deep End

Not all Black folk, but the ones I have thought to ask, share
a similar memory about their younger self being humbled
by a public pool— mine involves a 30-foot diving board
(the height increases every time I tell the story),
a neon swim cap & a light yet insistent push
from an 'instructor' plunging my six-year-old self
into conniption.

The surrounding spectators are a chorus of *oooof!*
Chlorine jabs each nostril— my limbs climbing to heaven
until an unrelenting hand pulls me into the safety
of a coughing fit— *I could have drowned* I exclaim
twenty something years later on the lazy river at Wet n Wild.

Let me start again— I cannot swim & I am not ashamed.
My mantra is simple: avoid the deep end. *We can teach you*
are my 'saviors" responses & I clapback with
Even the most capable fish can die if the water is poisoned.

Let me start again— I am certain the cause for my death
will be after my most aggressive fear is trivialized.
Every 'teacher' thinks they can save me
without knowing I drown daily.

The same thing that saves you might be
what pushed you into the deep end.
Call it darkness—so vast it becomes
unclear what to fight.

Inspired by Porsha Olayiwola

RECKLESS, TAQWA

Taqwa asks if
I want to be a man.
Lord no. Often, yes.
I was raised in a living room
with open invitation for Black men
in white socks to twist their knees to a
borrowed song they never plan to return
while sangin all the wrong words on purpose.
My dad, the lead singer— always wanna be Eddie
Kendricks cause Eddie smile the widest, so my daddy
sang with a full set of white teeth featuring a platinum molar
to play the part. Drinks his Red Stripe all the way to the moon
or the mud while his best friends be the rest of the Temptations,
any version will do. Sure, woman is too pretty of a name to call myself.
I deserve pretty things, but mostly 1960's soul. Run it. Are you a woman if

your father is all you ever wished to become?

Taqwa asks if I want to be a man. Lord yes. Often, no. My mother rocked a short cut
well before Whitney Houston taught us to *shoop*. I was raised by a woman who does
not need a special occasion to acquire a discount at the department store. Haggle
is such an ugly word, but damn if she don't question everyone, including the
State Attorney's Office if she don't feel like the price is just. Long live
the woman who deserted her childhood, helped take care of her
grandmother. Hollered the loudest at referees while never quite
knowing the rules of basketball. Yes, perhaps I wonder
woman things too, Taqwa. While spending more
at Macy's than my mother ever dreamt of,
Taqwa. Man is too reckless of a name
to call myself, though I deserve
reckless things, but mostly
family. Run it. Are you a
man if your mother
is all that you are
made of?

BLACK RAGE III: NOT FOR PROFIT

At this point it is highly unlikely for my communication
to be considered highly effective, so instead of counting
to ten I count how high my supervisor's salary can stretch
without high expectations for his presence at meetings.
The highest form of oppression usually presents itself
numerically. Statistically, I have a higher chance of demotion
if my confidence is perceived to be higher than hell.
High water is for higher tax bracket donors
who fund my face to look like I ain't got high blood
pressure from last week's meeting about how

staff morale needs to be higher.

ON DROWNING

At halftime, Coach Trish was always first to exit the court with a shouldered
power walk I believe only women in black pumps can achieve, before
disappearing into the darkest corner of the locker room. She found solace
while straddling a wooden bench, her back away from everything that owned
a mouth. At first listen, it could be mistaken as meditation, but a considerate
ear could easily detect her baying moans working too hard to silence
themselves. To be fair, it did not sound like a common cry, more like gasps
for air— an inconvenient time to drown nonetheless, & no one thought to ask
why, so often?

I cannot unsee her.

She was torn, then jailed in The Color Purple after refusing to apologize
with a fresh fist full of *hell no*. Peeped her on video screaming
Mama I love you! P - O - P hold it down in the back of a police car.
She was violently rocking back & forth at my cousin's funeral in the front
pew, & again at the reception while thanking everyone for coming.
When I ask her how can I help, she guards her heart while explaining,

Those tears had nothing to do with you. Nothing to do with right now.

I saw her in myself at my brother's wedding reception
when he stretched his arms just narrow enough
to hug me— refused to let me escape before ensuring I heard
him. When my brother repeats himself *I'm sorry. I'm sorry. I'm so sorry.*
I think of all he could have meant. The years we barely touched. The stitches
on my forehead. Every loss, like a kernel scratching in my throat to tears.
All the times I have longed to disappear into the darkest corner of the room.

For Us

This is for my people who learned to comb back & never curl
       with tapered pushbacks,
       double digit scars unhealed,
       untweezed brows.
If you want to learn our secrets, you must never leave our kitchens.
       When we say we burn here,
       we also mean we repeat
       our grandmothers' prayers.

This is for my people so soft
we can pull each other's eyelashes while two-steppin.
       Don't flinch.
       Trust we know hurt
       enough to be gentle.

This is for the packed suitcases in us, for us
       who give dap
       to men at bus stops
       who call us *queen*, our crowns
cracked before coronation. If our bodies are our homes,
our blood must be everywhere.

This is for ones who sat through high tea
       in black slacks,
       their necks draped
       in invisible pearls.
For the ones who throw a pinky finger to a sky
that ain't never loved us dry.

This is for the murdered Poussey in us.
The gunned down Cleo in us.
       Yes, you can try
       to grip that crowbar like a frisbee,
       aim it at our foreheads,
but we the kind only killed by love, so
       we may die today
       or live forever.

This is for the last time you came out to your parents
with a bottle of Malbec in your tears.
        The daylit park you got jumped in.
        The college team you got kicked off.
        The first time your thumb
met a splinter only your brother could pull out.

This is for me, how I dreamt of running
        til ankles
        disintegrated
        beneath me
— how far I meant to escape into a corn maze, so thick the sun
        no longer bothered to call,
        because this was where I thought
        my first kiss would be.

We, the first generation of ourselves allowed to embrace ourselves.
        This is for muddy-chinned smiles,
        unclenched fingers,
        coconut oil scalps,

flickering in the moonlight, begging darkness to notice the shine.

after Bao Phi

BALL IS LIFE

I chase the sky
as if it stole my wallet.
When it runs out of light,
I throne myself victorious.
After a peak of dawn demands
a rematch, I be like *the gall of this fool.*
I knew the world belonged to me when
my hands were mature enough to grip a man's
basketball on command, spread & planting the earth's
axis with fingers devouring its leather skin. My limbs no larger
than the day before, just more capable. Please don't mistake my
stubbornness as confidence. I was once a girl who assumed she could
dribble through a beehive of divorced men twice her size without a pinch.
Thirty-four stitches later & on my worst days, when I am no longer filled with light
& championships are foolish to desire, when I sprain my ankle from the couch, when
the number on my practice jersey fades, the mesh shrinks & I am too damn tired to stretch
before bedtime, I ask the clouds & their homies if they watched game tapes close enough
to see everything attempted. How can you say I gave up on this game if I wake up every
morning? Rebound every crooked opportunity? Nosedive into the most ungracious
occupations & risk losing all my teeth for a game with no scoreboard? How
can you say I gave up when I'm still standing, demanding to play?

My Neighbor Nash Say, Part IV

Ya know Teddy Pendergrass was damn
near suicidal after he got into that car
accident? I didnt mean to startle you but
ya know I always say lifes too short
to be pretendin a word aint what it was
meant for. When that depression
hit I heard thangs got so deep
his friends organized a fake funeral
to remind him he still had time to be loved.
Or at least loved beyond what he been
used to. Its wild when people refuse
to receive love in a different form
ya know? But I get it. Real insanity
is when ya forced to quit somethin
you feel you actually need. Hell.
Drug addiction sings that same tune.
I guess it would be different if you
was asked to quit somethin you hated.
Like a job. If someone forced me to quit
my job Id throw a party & bill it to HR.
No lie. I seen cats thinkin their lives cant
begin again after they leave this game.
You ever seen someone tear their ACL?
I know you seen a teammate
dislocate a bone but that dont count.
Thats a temporary injury. Ugly. But
temporary. Nah I mean a real break like
a meniscus or an achilles or sumthin.
When people bounce back from those
you imagine they belong to a church of sorts.
I guess folks just lucky out here sometimes too.
You know faith is the easiest thing
to sell? Mostly cause humans are naturally
favored. You ever seen someone find a quarter
on the sidewalk? Usually be a crusty lil thang too.
They pick it up rub it down then be like look
at gawd! As if there aint fools droppin

credit cards on accident every five minutes.
But if you have faith? Man you believe
a circumstance happened just for you.
Which is a pleasant notion I spose. A bit
selfish but I can dig it. So listen close
cause heres the real gravy. Everyone
will find what they love & they
will lose it. That is life. That is the seasoning
on the chicken. Its cooked.
Cant change it now. If you dont adjust
you will die hungry. I aint tryin to be dark
but man I remember for the longest time
I always wanted to sing cuz I loved
how music can be a personal time
machine. Yeah I played ball but sangin
was my real dream even though I struggled
to hold a note. Thought I was gonna be
like Teddy before that accident. On stage
with no air conditionin & drippin sweat
til someone carried me away. Trust this
wasnt about the women. Cuz I wasnt
dreamin about no women throwin panties
for me. Dats nasty. Truth be told
I was mostly in it for the lights. Those stage
lights be somethin else boy. Make you feel
like royalty. Like a hotel you feel good
stankin in. Find yo light kid. When it run out
find a new one. You eva wake up
without payin attention to the sky? Then
it just blooms like a petunia in heat?
Make you feel untied dont it?

LAST CALL

It is December in California, so by now the sun
is the houseguest who ate all your ice cream
down to the last spoonful

& I am walking the perimeter of a nearby park when
a young man approaches & I guess I refer to him as
young because instead of hollering he chose to run
like a newsie— his knees, like slinkys through a grass
field just to ask if I could join a game of three-on-three.

I am flattered & decline.

> *But we need you!*

& this is all I ever need to hear to make a poor decision.

I lace my walking shoes tight enough to convince
my doctor, *I made an effort*. Wonder which cylinder
of my back will ache by sunset & four games later—

> When I say I miss basketball I really mean
> the pick-up games, the courts with lines you
> can count on one hand, unbound by whistles,
> nobody betting against your body, no clock
> to check our ripeness, our prime. I miss the misfits
> who scream at the rim & never find answers.
>
> When we speak of utopia we are often saying
> there is already a world inside
> of this one we wish to live in.

It is winter in New England so by now black ice is
a next-door neighbor's eight-year-old child
with a fresh bag of glitter

& I am eight weeks old as a certified basketball
official in the state of Massachusetts.
Every time I place a uniform over my head
I feel powerful, as if I already know I rigged the game.

When I say all cops are bad cops what I mean is
you must have missed the last game I refereed.
Two athletically uninterested elementary schools,
the score: 0-4, two minutes left, & the only Black girl
on the court— the one who begged her teammates to pass
the rock for the past forty minutes— finally caught hold
of a rebound & held the ball with her entire stomach
wrapped around it. She curved her spine, extended her palm,
& stiff-armed everyone in sight like a running back. Shuffled
her feet without considering dribbling was a possibility, until
she reached the basket with bent aim.

& when I did not call *travel*, when I decided against
what has been taught in this sport since before I was born,
the spectators, often righteous in their sportsman-like persona,
were now belligerent. Outraged that I had the foresight
to decide this girl was beyond the rules
she had broken.

NOTES

My definition of an 'after' poem is when the new written work could never have existed without the previous brilliance, foresight, & talent of the original author.

With that said, I would first like to praise Ernest Gibson III for writing the original version of *Hold Me*, a poem I had often seen performed over a decade ago, & well before I considered myself a poet. My version of *Andragogy Or; Hold Me* aspires to jog alongside Gibson's creative stride— without intending to disrespect, imitate, or replicate his prowess. My only hope is to make him remotely proud.

A 'Vanguard' is a series of three poems connected in theme, subject matter & chronology; headed by a shorter 'vanguard' poem that introduces the reader to the series as a whole (four total poems). This form of poetry was founded by Amber Flame, & can be found in the poem(s) *Music of My Mind*. Thank you to Flame for the inspiration.

Black Rage I: A Colored Museum is inspired by George C. Wolfe's groundbreaking play *The Colored Museum* & more specifically, influenced by the line *'man kills his own rage...'*

Deep End is inspired by Porsha Olayiwola's poem entitled *Water*.

Some of the language used in *No One Said Don't Shoot* is inspired by Eve Ewing's series of poems of *Retellings*.

'I am Learning to Love Myself in Pieces' was originally entitled *Fragments*. The title is a quote from Jade Cho's poem entitled *Fragmentation*.

Bao Phi's original poem *For Us* can be found in a 2011 full length collection of poems entitled *Sông I Sing*, published by Coffeehouse Press. My version of the poem shifts perspective, but not form or repetition. Similar to *Hold Me*, this poem only has legs because of Phi's stellar poetic influence.

This is perhaps one of the most pretentious things I will write, & will later regret, but I am eager to mention the poem *When the Officer...* because it is an original bulleted-form poem. The hope is that you are able to read it in various ways. I thought it was kind of cool. So, anyway take a few options from 'plead' for example.

> *Plead, to god, to the waving baton, to the empty parking lot, Can I get a Witness? Who Made you this Brave? Am I dust to you? I want to believe in you. Find Belonging in someone else's hands. No one will be the same after this. Man listen, I want to be saved.*

Plead to God. Can I get a witness? I want to believe in you after this.

Plead to the waving baton, who made you this brave? Find belonging in someone else's hands.

_____ *& Basketball* was originally titled *Love & Basketball.* A previous version was graciously published by *FreezeRay Poetry* in July 2020.

For those wondering, Nash is a fantastical character. His voice is an eccentric culmination of Black men I grew up with, played ball with, & loved. His humor is based on my father's style of ridiculousness, but the name itself is based upon an older goggle wearing bald-headed Black man who would challenge me to a game of one-on-one almost every evening.

I have published & distributed three chapbooks: *Missed Layups, Sugar From a Honey Jar, & No Heaven for the House*— each collection contains earlier versions of poems written for *Lessons on Being Tenderheaded.*

ACKNOWLEDGMENTS

First, my mother & father would never forgive me if they were not thanked first & often for this collection. I was raised by two tremendous hearts. I hope they are as proud of me as I am of them. It is also important for me to admit, publicly, that my parents are & will continue to be my best friends.

Secondly, without Amber Flame this book would have never existed. No, you don't get it. It would have never been considered. She is a breathtaking author, musician & educator who held literal kegs of emotional labor throughout my writing & editing process. I am grateful for her friendship, partnership, & her ever evolving aptitude within the creative world. In case it is not listed, I would also consider her an official editor of this book.

Of course, thank you to the Write Bloody squad: Derrick Brown & Nikki Steele for believing, encouraging, & trusting my work. Thank you to my dope barber, Christian Eddings, for permission to edit their photo/image for the book cover art. Special praise to Wess 'Mongo' Jolley & Sam Preminger for being gentle, influential, & kick-ass editors.

In 2019, I was invited to perform as an opening act for the *Lord of the Butterflies* Tour, which prompted an exciting challenge— beginning a collection of poems to distribute, sell, & take pride in. Therefore, I owe a great deal of gratitude to Andrea Gibson & Megan Falley for the tour invitation & for encouraging me to finally believe my writing can be read & understood, rather than (solely) performed. Special thank you to Megan for being incredibly patient as my first official reader & editor— & prompting me to complete this sweet little honeypot of poems. Megan was the first to nominate my collection for publishing consideration.

An immense & sincere thank you to the following poets (in no particular order) who have inspired me over the years knowingly or unknowingly: Porsha Olayiola, Sarah O'Neal, Isabella Boregeson, Jade Cho, Gabriel Cortez, Natasha Huey, Ebony Stewart, Ariana Brown, Imani Cezanne, Darius Simpson, Sonya Renee Taylor, Melissa Lozada-Oliva, Jonathan Mendoza, Erich Hagan, Simone Beaubian, Tim 'Toaster' Henderson, Clint Smith, Amanda Torres, Hanif Abdurraqib, Pages Matam, William Giles, Christopher Diaz, Amir Safi, Javon Johnson, Ashley Davis, D. Ruff, Jha D, Eboni Hogan, J Mase III, Roya Marsh, Rachel Wiley, Ruby Alley, Jordan Peterson, Suzi Q. Smith, Denice Frohman, Sasha Banks, Will Evans, Zenaida Peterson, Tassiana Willis, Dominique Christina, Arvind Nadakumar, D'mani Thomas, Marissa Johnson, Larissa Melo, Nora Meiners, Rudy Francisco, Alyesha Wise, Letta Neely, Meaghan Ford, Melissa Newman Evans, Shannon

Matesky, Mckendy Fils Aime, Sean Patrick Mulroy, Golden, Carlynn Newhouse, Raych Jackson, Eve Ewing, Alan Pelaez Lopez, Marshall 'Gripp' Gilson, Aurielle Marie, Sam Sax, Khary Jackson, Tianna Bratcher, Ciera Jevae Gordon, Cecilia 'Cece' Jordan, Jeanann Verlee, Jason Henry Simon-Bierenbaum, Yujane Chen, Joshua Merchant, Kai Davis, Loyce Gayo, Sofia Snow, Elizabeth Acevedo, Tonya Ingram, Jamaica Osorio, Nate Marshall, Hannah Brown, Rob Gibsun, JR Mahung, Timothy DuWhite, Ashley August, Aleah Bradshaw, Tatiana Johnson-Boria, Justice Ameer Gaines, Chrysanthemum Tran, Paula Tran, Joshua Bennett, Ashley Haze, Theresa Davis, Theo Torre-de Castro, Bobby Crawford, Mikayla Mitchell, Quinn Edlin, Julian Randall, Mahogany L. Browne, Tongo Eisen Martin, Neiel Israel, Rudy Cabrera, Devin Samuels, Ken Arkind, Carrie Rudzinski, Kemi Alabi, Sandy Lopez & Omoizele 'Oz' Okoawo. Everyone I failed to name is still incredible. Forgive me.

Shout out to Boston, MA. Shout out to Petersburg, VA. Shout out to Newark, DE. Shout out to Oakland, CA. Shout out to Elk Grove/Sacramento, CA. Shout out to Tacoma, WA. Shout out to community venues who provide us with second homes & continuously empower generations of creatives. Shout out to my people who are uninterested in poetry, yet decided to give this book the good ol' college try. Shout out to Zeta Phi Beta Sorority Inc. & the Epsilon Rho Zeta Chapter. Shout out to my former teammates & coaches. Shout out to Haley House, Bella Luna Cafe, Cantab Lounge, MLK Cafe, Neighborly, & Red Bay Coffee. Shout out to Button Poetry, Write About Now, & Slamfind for respectfully publishing my older performances.

Once again, I want to thank my family (all dem): Donna Johnon, Archie Johnson, Aaron Johnson, Diana Johnson, Amaya Janae Johnson, Aaron Johnson II, Aaron Wilson, Terrence Boyd Jr., Rosa Evans, Vanisha Boyd, Kendra Carr, Samuel Carr Sr., Terrence Boyd Sr., Trina Norris, Tabia Norris, Sharifa Norris, Andrew 'Spider' Norris, Amber Boyd, Breanna Boyd, Pam Breckenridge, Brenda Beaugard, Timothy Boyd, Sydney Boyd, Basil Boyd, Ashley Ford, Jamila Adams, Mark Adams, Felicia Brown, Albrey Brown, Andrea Jones, Clifford Jones, Mark Boyd, Doroline Boyd, Saundra 'Rene' Gaston Hammonds, Alexandria Gaston, Liz Gaston, Kevin Johnson, Nathaniel Johnson Jr., Jamal Johnson, Lamar Johnson, Rachel Ortega, Jewel Johnson, Maya Johnson & Ruby Bristo. A few members of my first chosen family are Robbin Coaxum, Paul Coaxum Sr., Paul Coaxum Jr., Brian Coaxum & the cousins, elders, siblings or descendants of each individual of the names listed above.

Rest in peace: Abel Boyd, Nakeba Johnson, Kermit Johnson, Nathaniel Johnson Sr., Luther 'June' Johnson Jr., Luther Johnson Sr., Elnora Johnson, Lillian Brown, David Sims & my grandmother, Elouise Johnson. May your legacy live on through this gentle remembrance & beyond.

Please understand, everything I write is for Black folk. Then for Queer folk. If you are both folk, you are lovely, beautiful, & deserve a miracle. Everyone else is a witness.

If you read this book in its entirety, I love you. Thank you for your support.

ABOUT THE AUTHOR

JANAE JOHNSON (she/her) is an award-winning poet, performer, educator, curator, and DJ with a collection of work that celebrates Black queer masculinity, kinship, and belonging. She is a National Poetry Slam Champion, Women of the World Poetry Slam Champion, and a founder of two nationally recognized poetry venues: The Root Slam (Oakland, CA) and The House Slam (Boston, MA). Her work has been featured in multiple outlets such as *PBS NewsHour*, *ESPNW*, and *FreezeRay Poetry*. Janae holds a M.Ed in Educational Leadership and currently facilitates writing workshops for incarcerated and justice-impacted women and youth.

IF YOU LIKE JANAE JOHNSON, JANAE LIKES...

The Heart of a Comet
Pages Matam

Ordinary Cruelty
Amber Flame

Pecking Order
Nicole Homer

Counting Descent
Clint Smith

Any Psalm You Want
Khary Jackson

WRITEBLOODY
QUALITY AMERICAN BOOKS

Write Bloody Publishing publishes and promotes great books of poetry every year.
We believe that poetry can change the world for the better. We are an independent press
dedicated to quality literature and book design, with an office
in Los Angeles, California.

We are grassroots, DIY, bootstrap believers. Pull up a good book and join the family.
Support independent authors, artists, and presses.

Want to know more about Write Bloody books, authors, and events?
Join our mailing list at

www.writebloody.com

Write Bloody Books

CPSIA information can be obtained
at www.ICGtesting.com
Printed in the USA
JSHW030141250322
24107JS00005B/22